ma+h
EVERYWHERE!

SHOPPING TRIP MATH

KATIE MARSICO

Lerner Publications Company • Minneapolis

To my editor, Ashley, and all the other wonderful
staff at Lerner

Lerner Publications Company
A division of Lerner Publishing Group, Inc.
241 First Avenue North
Minneapolis, MN 55401 USA

For reading levels and more information, look up this title at www.lernerbooks.com.

Photo Acknowledgments
The images in this book are used with the permission of: © iStockphoto.com/piksel, p. 1; © White Packert/The Image Bank/ Getty Images, p. 4; © iStockphoto.com/eldacarin, p. 5 (coins); © iStockphoto.com/spxChrome, pp. 5, 9, 11, 15, 17, 21, 23, 25 (notebook paper); © iStockphoto.com/alubalish, pp. 5, 9, 11, 15, 21, 27 (torn paper); © Tanya Constantine/Blend Images/ Thinkstock, p. 6;© JNP/Shutterstock.com, p. 7; © iStockphoto.com/stevecoleimages, p. 8; © iStockphoto.com/mehmettorlak, p. 9 (birdseed); © iStockphoto.com/LattaPictures, p. 10; © Marv Johnson/FogStock/Thinkstock, p. 12; © iStockphoto.com/ cunfek, p. 13; © Terry Vine/Blend Images/Thinkstock, p. 14; © Joingate/Dreamstime.com, p. 15 (balloon); © Stock Connection/ SuperStock, p. 16; © Sam Aronov/Shutterstock.com, p. 17 (comic books); © Hill Street Studios/Blend Images/Getty Images, p. 18; © iStockphoto.com/toomler, p. 19 (paint streaks); © iStockphoto.com/hidesy, p. 19 (paint buckets); © iStockphoto.com/ Juanmonino, p. 20; © iStockphoto.com/Elenarts, p. 21 (shirts); © Jeff Greenberg/Alamy, p. 22; © Mrsiraphol/Shutterstock. com, p. 23 (notebooks); © Juice Images/Alamy, p. 24; © iStockphoto.com/HSNPhotography, p. 25 (dvds); © Pavel L. Photo and Video/Shutterstock.com, p. 26; © Portokalis/Shutterstock.com, p. 27 (beads); © iStockphoto.com/andylid, p. 28; © VeryOlive/Shutterstock.com, p. 29.

Front Cover: © iStockphoto.com/Ljupco (shopping cart), © iStockphoto.com/rusmor (graph paper).
Back Cover: © iStockphoto.com/mattjeacock.

Main body text set in Conduit ITC Std 14/18. Typeface provided by International Typeface Corp.

Library of Congress Cataloging-in-Publication Data

Marsico, Katie, 1980– author
        Shopping trip math / by Katie Marsico.
            pages   cm — (Math everywhere!)
        Includes index.
        ISBN 978–1–4677–1884–4 (lib. bdg. : alk. paper)
        ISBN 978–1–4677–4697–7 (eBook)
            1. Mathematics—Juvenile literature. 2. Problem solving—Juvenile literature.
        3. Shopping—Juvenile literature. 4. Money—Juvenile literature. I. Title.
        QA40.5.M3775 2015
        513—dc23   2013046315

Manufactured in the United States of America
1 – CG – 7/15/14

TABLE OF CONTENTS

CHANGE FOR CHOCOLATE

Math isn't just about questions on quizzes and homework. It shapes the entire world around us. Want to know how? Simply head to the store!

That's where Alex and his cousin Joe hope to go. They're craving candy! Alex asks their grandma if they can walk to the candy shop on the corner. She agrees. Of course, she also makes them promise they won't spoil their appetite before dinner.

The cousins gather some change for chocolate. Alex empties his piggy bank. He has 15 quarters, 11 dimes, 16 nickels, and 14 pennies. That should be enough to satisfy each cousin's sweet tooth.

Alex and Joe face some tough but tasty choices at the candy shop. In the end, they decide on chocolate-covered raisins. They also want chocolate-covered almonds. Raisins are $5.99 per pound. Almonds are $7.99 per pound.

Alex and Joe scoop ½ pound (227 grams) of raisins into a bag. **How much will this cost? What if they decide to spend the rest of their money on the biggest bag of almonds they can afford? How much would it weigh?** (Round to the nearest hundredth of a pound.)

DO THE MATH!

You head to the vending machine at the front of the candy shop. For 25¢, you can enjoy a big, juicy gumball. The problem is that you have a dollar bill. And the machine only takes quarters. You ask the store owner to give you change for $1. He hands you a dime and three nickels. The rest of your change is in quarters. How many gumballs can you get?

Check your answers to all questions on pages 30–31.

PAY FOR A WINTER WARDROBE

Brrr! Quinn's teeth are chattering as she hurries into the mall. It won't be long before snow starts falling! That's why Quinn and her dad are going shopping. They plan to stock up on warm winter clothes.

Quinn can't wait to hit her favorite stores. Yet she has to pay attention to prices. Her dad says she has $150 to spend on a new winter wardrobe. Quinn's rich, right? Well, it depends. Winter fashion can be expensive!

Quinn needs more sweaters. Her dad says she could use at least two new pairs of long pants. She also has to get a scarf, a hat, and a coat.

Quinn keeps cost in mind as she moves through the mall. First, she buys two stylish sweaters. One is $16.99. The other is $14.39. Next, she purchases a hat for $9.99. Her dad finds matching gloves for $7.99. The scarf Quinn chooses is $12.99. So far, so good!

But picking pants and a coat is trickier. Quinn likes three pairs of pants. Each one is $16.99. Meanwhile, the coat Quinn wants is $39.99. **Can she afford the coat *and* all three pairs of pants?**

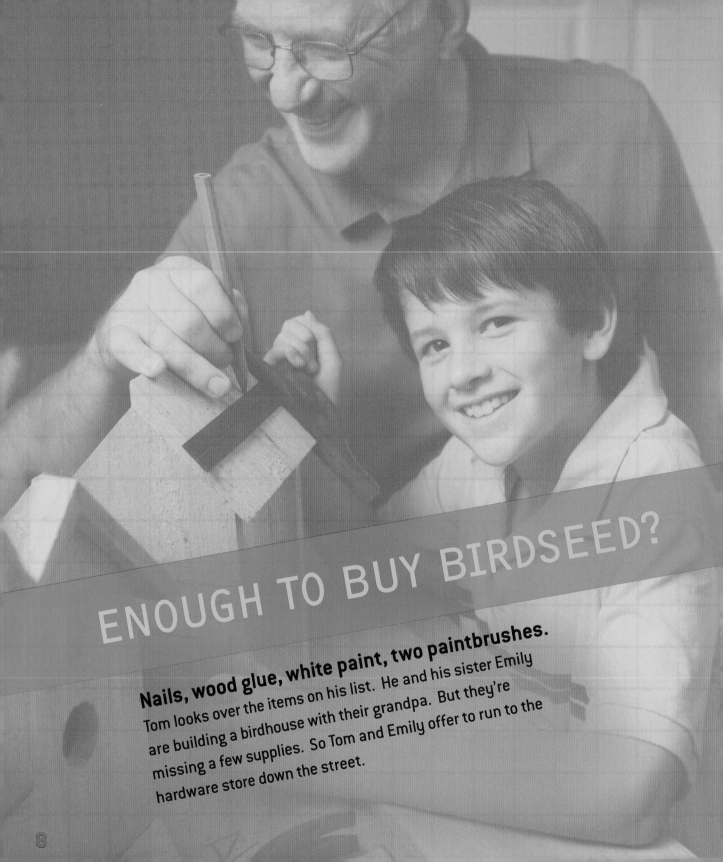

ENOUGH TO BUY BIRDSEED?

Nails, wood glue, white paint, two paintbrushes. Tom looks over the items on his list. He and his sister Emily are building a birdhouse with their grandpa. But they're missing a few supplies. So Tom and Emily offer to run to the hardware store down the street.

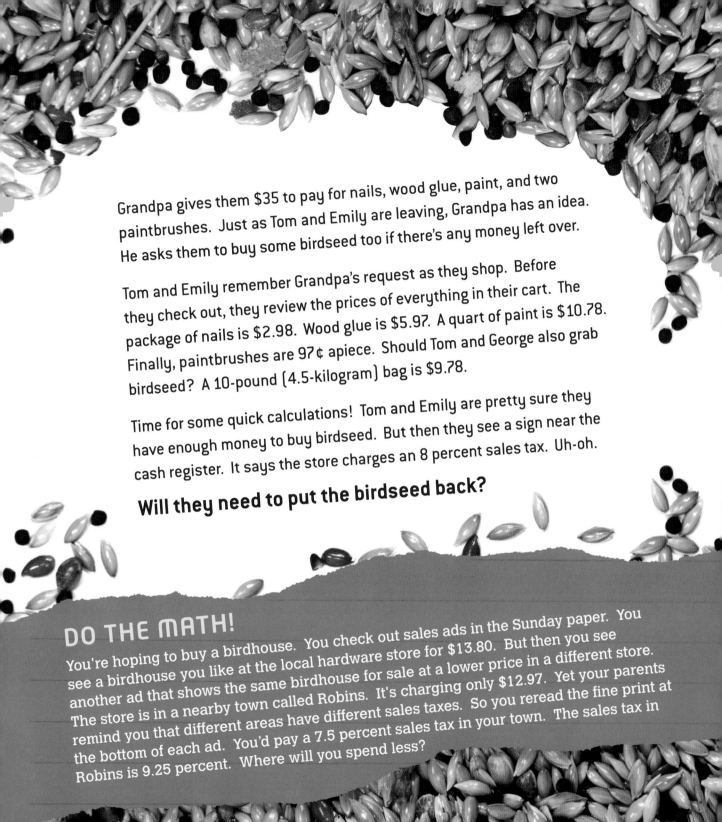

Grandpa gives them $35 to pay for nails, wood glue, paint, and two paintbrushes. Just as Tom and Emily are leaving, Grandpa has an idea. He asks them to buy some birdseed too if there's any money left over.

Tom and Emily remember Grandpa's request as they shop. Before they check out, they review the prices of everything in their cart. The package of nails is $2.98. Wood glue is $5.97. A quart of paint is $10.78. Finally, paintbrushes are 97¢ apiece. Should Tom and George also grab birdseed? A 10-pound (4.5-kilogram) bag is $9.78.

Time for some quick calculations! Tom and Emily are pretty sure they have enough money to buy birdseed. But then they see a sign near the cash register. It says the store charges an 8 percent sales tax. Uh-oh.

Will they need to put the birdseed back?

DO THE MATH!

You're hoping to buy a birdhouse. You check out sales ads in the Sunday paper. You see a birdhouse you like at the local hardware store for $13.80. But then you see another ad that shows the same birdhouse for sale at a lower price in a different store. The store is in a nearby town called Robins. It's charging only $12.97. Yet your parents remind you that different areas have different sales taxes. So you reread the fine print at the bottom of each ad. You'd pay a 7.5 percent sales tax in your town. The sales tax in Robins is 9.25 percent. Where will you spend less?

SHOPPING AND SHIPPING

Keira is ready to redo her room! Her sister just moved to college. That means Keira is finally free to decorate her way. Her mom and dad still have to okay her choices, though.

Mom suggests they get ideas online. So Keira scrolls through a few websites. Before long, she spots the perfect bedding set! It's got her favorite colors—pink and green.

Keira also sees cool accessories on two other sites. Her room would look awesome with a lava lamp. Wall decals would be a nice touch too.

The price of the bedding set is $59.99. The lamp Keira likes is $13.49. The wall decals she wants are $12.99. Keira is ready to place an order online!

Her parents aren't so sure, though. After all, those prices don't include shipping and handling. Online shopping might be easier than going to different stores in person. But it's not always cheaper.

Keira checks the extra fee for each item. Shipping and handling comes to $10.49 for the bedding set. It's $6.49 for the lava lamp. It would be $4.49 for the wall decals.

The lamp and decals have the same sales prices at the local stores as they do online. But the bedding set on the website is part of an online special. So it's $10 cheaper than it would be at the store.

How much will Keira spend if she orders everything online? How does it compare to what she'd pay at the stores?

DO THE MATH!

Time for a little online shopping! You're doing some browsing with a trusted adult. You want to buy posters for your bedroom. All three posters you like are available through the same site. Two are $13.50. The third is $19.85. This week, the poster store is running an online special. If you spend $50 or more, you get free shipping. If not, there's an $8.99 shipping fee. How much will you pay for your posters?

11

BORROW AT THE BOOKSTORE

What's better than a trip to the bookstore? Not much, if you ask Jason. He loves reading. His bookshelf is almost full. But he hopes to make room for two more books.

His two favorite authors have just published new mysteries. The waiting list at the library is superlong for both books. So Jason's mom offers to take him to the bookstore. Before they leave, he grabs the money he's been saving up.

Jason has $21 in his pocket, thanks to the allowance he gets from doing chores. He earns $3 every time he rakes leaves. He also helps his mom sweep and vacuum. She pays Jason 50¢ for each room he cleans.

There's good news and bad news once Jason gets to the bookstore. The good news: he snags the last copy of each book. The bad news: he's a bit short on cash. The first book is $15.47. The second is $13.30.

Jason can't decide which book to choose! Luckily, his mom comes to the rescue. She tells Jason she'll lend him some money. He can pay her back by doing a few extra chores.

For starters, their lawn needs to be raked. So does his grandparents' yard. And Jason's mom is hosting a big family party this Saturday. She wants to tidy up the house before then.

Jason promises his mom he'll rake both yards. He'll have to do a little vacuuming and sweeping to pay back the rest of the money. **How many rooms will he need to clean?**

PARTY PURCHASES

It's party time! Stephanie and Aunt Jen are planning a super celebration. They're surprising Uncle Jaime for his birthday. And what birthday bash is complete without balloons?

Aunt Jen needs to pop in at the party store. Stephanie goes with her. Before shopping, they discuss their budget. Aunt Jen says they can spend about $25 on balloons. She puts Stephanie in charge of picking them out. Meanwhile, Aunt Jen heads to another aisle to look for party favors.

First, Stephanie chooses five star-shaped balloons. Each costs $1.99. She also grabs two packages of smaller balloons to blow up later. Each package is $4.99.

Stephanie thinks she's done. But then she spots something Uncle Jaime would adore! It's a giant balloon in the shape of a football. Stephanie knows Uncle Jaime is a huge football fan. She also knows that Aunt Jen set a balloon budget, though.

The floating football is $6.99. That would put Stephanie over her price limit. So she decides to get the football balloon instead of some of the star-shaped balloons. **How many star-shaped balloons should she put back?**

DO THE MATH!

You're going to Uncle Jaime's party too! You decide to get him a football jersey for his birthday. The jersey is $27.12. Should you order it online? Today is Monday. The party is this Sunday, six days from now. If you use standard shipping, you'll have the jersey in three to five business days. Business days are Monday through Friday. The standard shipping fee is $5.58. Two-day shipping guarantees faster delivery. You'll have the jersey in two business days. You'll also pay $12.24. Which shipping method should you use? How much will you end up paying altogether?

SHOULD THE SET BE SPLIT?

Mr. Brown's resale shop is like a giant treasure trove. Jake never knows what he'll discover there. Mr. Brown has everything from fishing poles to used books to baseball cards. Today, Jake stumbles upon his most amazing find yet. It's a run of 12 comic books! And they just happen to be some of Jake's favorites.

Mr. Brown is asking $26.50 for the entire set. Jake can't argue that the price is a steal. But he's not positive about making a purchase because he already owns four books in the run.

Fortunately, Mr. Brown is flexible. He says he can split up the set. Jake knows that he wants eight of the books.

He reasons that $26.50 ÷ 12 = $2.21.

So he's ready to pay Mr. Brown $2.21 per comic book.

But Mr. Brown explains that it's not quite that simple. The comics are easier for him to sell when they're part of a complete set. So if Mr. Brown separates them, he'll have to charge slightly more per book.

He's willing to sell individual issues for $3.15 each. Jake considers his offer.

How much would he save by buying only eight comic books?

THINK ABOUT THE BIG PICTURE

Marisa is ready to liven up the school lunchroom! She's president of the art club. The club's big project for the year is to paint a mural in the cafeteria. A few weeks ago, club members organized a bake sale and earned $100 to spend on their artistic efforts.

Marisa and Ms. Wells, the art teacher, head out to buy their first batch of paint. They hope to make their money stretch a long way.

The mural's main background color will be purple. Marisa and Ms. Wells will need enough purple paint to cover one of the cafeteria's walls. So Marisa checks out different brands of purple paint. The first brand costs $18.95 per quart. The second runs $35.96 a gallon. Marisa likes the look of the lower number. But she'd get more paint if she went with the second brand.

Marisa knows that 1 gallon (3.8 liters) = 4 quarts (3.8 L).

Ms. Wells says they should decide between brands based on unit price. That involves figuring out the cost per quart. If Marisa needed just 1 quart (950 milliliters) of paint, it would make sense to simply pay $18.95. But she has to think about the big picture. It'll take more than a quart to cover the cafeteria wall. In fact, Ms. Wells estimates they'll end up using about 8 quarts (7.6 L).

What is the unit price of the second brand of purple paint? How does it compare to the unit price of the first brand? How much will it cost to buy 8 quarts (7.6 L) of whichever brand is the better deal?

WHAT'S FOR FREE?

Ready for some Saturday shopping? Ben is . . . kind of. His mom takes him to the mall to look for new shirts. Ben would prefer to buy video games. But his closet could use a little sprucing up.

Today is the day to do it too! The biggest clothing store at the mall is running a special sale. A sign in the window says, "Buy two shirts and get a third shirt of equal or lesser value free!"

Ben and his mom get to work. Together, they pick out six shirts. Two have cool logos. Those are each $16.50. The third shirt features Ben's favorite cartoon characters. It's $12.99.

The fourth and fifth shirts are pretty formal. Ben thinks they're kind of boring. But his mom says they'll be good for holiday parties and class pictures. Those shirts are $25 and $35. The last shirt is $19.97. It's made of warm flannel. Ben wants to wear it to the football game tomorrow.

At last, it's time to check out. Ben's mom explains that because of how the sale is organized, only the cheapest shirts will be free. **How many shirts will Ben get for free? What will his total bill be?**

DO THE MATH!

Your aunt just gave you a sweater. Unfortunately, it's the wrong size. Good thing you have a gift receipt! You head to the store where she bought it. You plan to exchange the sweater for something else. The clerk says you have $34.95 in store credit. She also mentions that the store is having a sale. If you buy one sweater, you'll get another at half price. The second sweater must be of equal or lesser value. The first sweater you choose is $26.95. The second is $21.99. How much will you spend after you've applied your store credit?

SAVE ON SPIRALS

So long, summer break! Hello, new school year! Olivia just got a letter and a school supply list from her new teacher.

Some kids like buying clothes. Others get excited about a trip to the toy store. But Olivia is nuts about back-to-school shopping. She loves picking out folders with cool designs. Then there's the joy of looking for the perfect lunch box.

Olivia is ready to shop, label, and get organized. But her mom tells her to hold tight. She shows Olivia a newspaper ad for a local office supply store. A big sale starts Friday. School supplies will be 25 percent off!

The teacher's note says Olivia will need six folders and two spiral notebooks. She also has to buy 24 pencils and four large erasers.

Normally, folders are 77¢ each at the store. Spirals are $1.49 apiece. A package of 24 pencils is $6.49. One eraser is usually 49¢. **What will each of these items cost on Friday? How much will Olivia save if she waits until Friday to buy folders, spirals, pencils, and erasers?**

A DVD DEAL

Will wants to move to Hollywood someday. He dreams of becoming an actor or a big-name director. So how can he prepare for this amazing career? By viewing as many movies as possible!

Today, Will and Uncle Pete are strolling through the home entertainment section of the department store. They spot a big bin of DVDs. The sign next to it says the store is running a special on DVDs. What better time to build Will's film collection?

Each movie in the bin is $5. Or a customer can buy four for $18. Will and Uncle Pete start filling their cart. Uncle Pete says Will can repay him later—when he's rich and famous.

Will is on the fence about two films. He likes both movies. But he's not sure how often he'd watch them. Besides, Will wants to be practical. It might be a while before he's well known in Hollywood. He doesn't want to take too long to repay his uncle.

How much will Uncle Pete save per DVD if he buys eight? How much will he spend if he purchases 10?

Few presents beat a gift card for the toy store. At least that's what Nicole thinks. She just got a $30 gift card for her birthday. Nicole's older sister Sadie is driving her to the toy store this morning. Before they go, their mom gives Nicole two coupons she found online.

One coupon is for 10 percent off a person's entire purchase. The other is for 15 percent off a single item. Wait a second, though! What's that fine print at the bottom of the second coupon? Nicole reads it carefully. The discount only applies to a single toy that cost $25 or less.

Nicole thanks her mom. She's not sure which coupon she'll use. But she's certain that either one will be a big help.

At the store, Nicole makes a beeline for the craft aisle. The bracelet-making kit she wants is $15.49. The necklace-making kit she picks out is $13.59.

Nicole hands the clerk her gift card. Should she present both her coupons? The clerk says no. There's a limit of one coupon per person. Oh, and the 15 percent discount applies to a customer's least expensive item.

Nicole wants to spend as little as possible. **Which coupon should she use today? Will there be any money left on her gift card?**

DO THE MATH!

You're a loyal customer of two different toy stores. You've been using a gift card at the first one. There's $5.45 left on it. You also have a 20 percent off coupon for this store. It's good on any single item under $50. Meanwhile, you have a 30 percent off coupon for the second store. It applies to your entire purchase. Both stores carry the same remote-controlled robot. Both are selling it for $49.99. You're determined to buy it! Where will you spend the least?

READY, SET, SHOP!

Are you all set to hit your favorite store? Your new math skills will come in handy as you shop! Besides, isn't there a big sale starting tomorrow? But first, you need to solve some final problems.

Who knew that shopping for a pet could be so complex? You and your brother plan to adopt two baby hamsters. Before heading to the shelter to pick up the pets, you stop at the pet store to get pet-care supplies. You'll need to buy two cages and a few other items.

You notice that the store sells a hamster "starter kit." It costs $28.79. The kit includes a cage, a water bottle, a food dish, and a wheel. It also comes with two treat sticks and 1 pound (450 g) of food. The clerk tells you the food should last each hamster about two weeks. The kit contains 10 ounces (280 g) of bedding too. That's enough to fill the cage.

You can buy the exact same cage—without all the supplies—for $17.42. It's still equipped with a water bottle, a food dish, and a wheel. But you'd have to purchase everything else separately. The store carries a 3-pound (1.4 kg) bag of food for $7.37. There's also a 50 percent off sale on treat sticks. The normal price for a package of four is $6.99. Finally, a 3-pound bag of bedding is $4.49.

How much will you pay for two starter kits? How about if you buy the cages and supplies separately?

Don't forget to consider overall value too! **How often can you fill each cage using a 3-pound (1.4 kg) bag of bedding?** (To compare how long different-sized bags will last, you'll need to convert weight to a single unit.)

How soon will your hamsters finish 3 pounds (1.4 kg) of food?

Remember that 1 pound (450 g) = 16 ounces.

Answer Key

Page 5   The cost of ½ pound (227 g) of chocolate-covered raisins is $3. (½ lb. × $5.99 per lb. = $2.995, or about $3)
The biggest bag of chocolate-covered almonds Alex and Joe can afford weighs 0.35 pounds (159 g). (15 quarters × $0.25 = $3.75; 11 dimes × $0.10 = $1.10; 16 nickels × $0.05 = $0.80; 14 pennies × $0.01 = $0.14; $3.75 + $1.10 + $0.80 + $0.14 = $5.79; $5.79 − $3 for raisins = $2.79; $2.79 ÷ $7.99 per lb. = 0.349 lbs., which rounds to 0.35 lbs.)

Do the Math!
You can get three gumballs. (1 dime × $0.10 = $0.10; 3 nickels × $0.05 = $0.15; $0.10 + $0.15 = $0.25; $1 − $0.25 = $0.75; $0.75 ÷ $0.25 per gumball = 3 gumballs)

Page 7   Quinn can't afford the coat and all three pairs of pants. ($16.99 + $14.39 + $9.99 + $7.99 + $12.99 + $39.99 = $102.34; $150 − $102.34 = $47.66; $47.66 ÷ $16.99 per pair of pants = 2.805 pairs of pants, which is less than 3 pairs of pants)

Page 9   Tom and George will not need to put the birdseed back. ($2.98 + $5.97 + $10.78 = $19.73; 2 brushes × $0.97 per brush = $1.94; $19.73 + $1.94 + $9.78 = $31.45; $31.45 × 0.08 sales tax = $2.52; $31.45 + $2.52 = $33.97, which is less than $35)

Do the Math!
You would spend less in Robins. ($13.80 × 0.075 = $1.04; $13.80 + $1.04 = $14.84; $12.97 × 0.0925 = $1.20; $12.97 + $1.20 = $14.17)

Page 11   Keira will spend $107.94 ordering everything online. ($59.99 + $13.49 + $12.99 = $86.47; $86.47 + $10.49 + $6.49 + $4.49 = $107.94)
It's $11.47 more than what she'd pay in stores. ($59.99 + $10 = $69.99; $69.99 + $13.49 + $12.99 = $96.47; $107.94 − $96.47 = $11.47)

Do the Math!
You'll pay $55.84 for your posters. (2 posters × $13.50 per poster = $27; $27 + $19.85 = $46.85, which is less than $50; $46.85 + $8.99 = $55.84)

Page 13   Jason will have to clean four rooms. ($15.47 + $13.30 = $28.77; $28.77 − $21 = $7.77; 2 yards × $3 per yard = $6; $7.77 − $6 = $1.77; $1.77 ÷ $0.50 per room = 3.54 rooms, or about 4 rooms)

Page 15   Stephanie should put one star-shaped balloon back. (5 star-shaped balloons × $1.99 per star-shaped balloon = $9.95; 2 packages of smaller balloons × $4.99 per package = $9.98; $9.95 + $9.98 + $6.99 = $26.92; $26.92 − $25 = $1.92; $1.92 ÷ $1.99 per star-shaped balloon = 0.96 star-shaped balloon, or about 1 star-shaped balloon)

Do the Math!
If you use standard shipping, you might get the jersey Thursday, April 10; Friday, April 11; or Monday, April 14. This last date falls after the party. So you should probably play it safe and use two-day shipping. (Monday, 4/7, + 3 business days = Thursday, 4/10; Monday, 4/7, + 4 business days = Friday, 4/11; Monday, 4/7, + 5 business days = Monday, 4/14)
Uncle Jaime's gift will cost $39.36 ($27.12 + $12.24 = $39.36)

Page 17   Jake would save $1.30 buying only eight comic books. ($3.15 per comic book × 8 comic books = $25.20; $26.50 − $25.20 = $1.30)

Page 19 The unit price of the second brand of purple paint is $8.99 per quart. ($35.96 per gal./4 qts. ÷ 4 qts. = $8.99 per qt.)

It's $9.96 less than the unit price of the first brand. ($18.95 − $8.99 = $9.96)

It will cost $71.92 to buy 8 quarts (7.6 L) of the second brand of purple paint. (8 qts. ÷ 4 qts. per can = 2 cans; 2 cans × $35.96 per can = $71.92)

Page 21 Ben will get two shirts for free. (6 shirts ÷ 3 shirts per sale group = 2 free shirts)

His total bill will be $96.47. ($16.50 + $25 + $35 + $19.97 = $96.47)

Do the Math!

You will spend $3 today. (½ × $21.99 = $10.995, which rounds to $11; $11 + $26.95 = $37.95; $37.95 − $34.95 = $3)

Page 23 Folders will cost 58¢ on Friday. (0.25 × $0.77 = $0.193, or about $0.19; $0.77 − $0.19 = $0.58). Spirals will cost $1.12 on Friday. (0.25 × $1.49 = $0.373, or about $0.37; $1.49 − $0.37 = $1.12). A package of 24 pencils will cost $4.87 on Friday. (0.25 × $6.49 = $1.623, or about $1.62; $6.49 − $1.62 = $4.87). An eraser will cost 37¢ on Friday. (0.25× $0.49 = $0.123, or about $0.12; $0.49 − $0.12 = $0.37).

Olivia will save $3.98 if she waits to buy folders, spirals, pencils, and erasers. (6 folders × $0.77 per folder = $4.62; 2 spirals × $1.49 per spiral = $2.98; 1 package of pencils × $6.49 per package = $6.49; 4 erasers × $0.49 per eraser = $1.96; $4.62 + $2.98 + $6.49 + $1.96 = $16.05; 6 folders × $0.58 per folder = $3.48; 2 spirals × $1.12 per spiral = $2.24; 1 package of pencils × $4.87 per package = $4.87; 4 erasers × $0.37 per eraser = $1.48; $3.48 + $2.24 + $4.87 + $1.48 = $12.07; $16.05 − $12.07 = $3.98)

Page 25 Uncle Pete will save 50¢ per DVD if he buys eight. (8 DVDs ÷ 4 DVDs per sale group = 2 sale groups; 2 sale groups × $18 per sale group = $36; $36 ÷ 8 DVDs = $4.50 per DVD; $5 − $4.50 = $0.50)

He'll spend $46 if he purchases 10 DVDs. ($18 per sale group ÷ 4 DVDs per sale group = $4.50 per DVD; $4.50 × 8 DVDs that qualify for the sale = $36; $5 × 2 DVDs that don't qualify for the sale = $10; $36 + $10 = $46)

Page 27 Nicole should use the coupon for 10 percent off her entire purchase. ($15.49 + $13.59 = $29.08; $29.08 × 0.10 = $2.908, which rounds to $2.91; $29.08 − $2.91 = $26.17; $13.59 × 0.15 = $2.039, which rounds to $2.04; $13.59 − $2.04 = $11.55; $15.49 + $11.55 = $27.04)

She'll have $3.83 left on her gift card. ($30 − $26.17 = $3.83)

Do the Math!

You'll spend the least at the first store. ($49.99 × 0.20 = $9.998, or about $10; $10 + $5.45 = $15.45; $49.99 − $15.45 = $34.54; $49.99 × 0.30 = $14.997, or about $15; $49.99 − $15 = $34.99)

Page 29 Ready, Set, Shop!

You'll pay $57.58 for two starter kits. ($28.79 per starter kit × 2 starter kits = $57.58)

You'll pay $50.20 if you buy the cages and supplies separately. ($17.42 per cage × 2 cages = $34.84; 0.50 × $6.99 = $3.495, or about $3.50; $34.84 + $3.50 + $7.37 + $4.49 = $50.20)

You can fill each cage about two times using a 3-pound (1.4 kg) bag of bedding. (3 lbs. × 16 oz. per pound = 48 oz.; 48 oz. of bedding ÷ 10 oz. to fill 1 cage = 4.8 times that 1 cage can be filled; 4.8 times 1 cage can be filled ÷ 2 cages = 2.4 times, or about 2 times that 2 cages can be filled)

Your hamsters will finish 3 pounds (1.4 kg) of food in 1.5 weeks. (3 lbs. ÷ 1 lb. per week per hamster = 3 weeks per hamster; 3 weeks per hamster ÷ 2 hamsters = 1.5 weeks)

Glossary

browsing: looking over various goods for sale

budget: the amount of money available for a specific purpose

calculation: the result of using math to figure out the number or amount of something

clerk: a person who works in a store

department store: a large store that sells many different kinds of goods

discount: a reduction in the usual price of something

gift card: a card that allows the recipient to receive goods or services of a specified value from a certain store

sales tax: money, usually a percentage of an item's price, that a store collects on each purchase

unit price: how much an item costs per an individual unit of measurement

Further Information

Furgang, Kathy. *National Geographic Kids Everything Money: A Wealth of Facts, Photos, and Fun!* Washington, DC: National Geographic Children's Books, 2013. Find out how money is made, saved, and spent all around the world.

IXL Learning—Third Grade
http://www.ixl.com/math/grade-3
Head to this site for practice problems that focus on many of the math topics you've just learned about.

Larson, Jennifer S. *Who's Buying? Who's Selling? Understanding Consumers and Producers.* Minneapolis: Lerner Publications, 2010. Learn more about how people work together to buy and sell things in the marketplace.

Oink
http://oink.com
Talk to a parent or a guardian about setting up a free account with Oink if you're looking for real-life experience shopping, saving, and managing money.

Index